notes

to a

leader

Michael Weatherspoon

KEEN VISION PUBLISHING

Notes to a Leader
Copyright © 2020 by Michael J. Weatherspoon

Requests for permissions should be electronically mailed to themaverick@keen-vision.com

Cover Design: Justin James (Envisage Media Consulting)

Printed in the United States of America

Keen Vision Publishing, LLC
www.keen-vision.com
ISBN: 978-1-948270-57-1

For my loving mother, Ethel Mae Weatherspoon and my precious and amazing daughter, Mackenzie Janai' Weatherspoon.

contents

foreword

If you shop at any reputable bookstore, search your favorite sites online, scroll LinkedIn, watch YouTube and Instagram, or follow thought leaders, you will see and find more than your fair share of materials on leadership from the millions of posts, articles, and books on the subject. Within those, you will find millions of philosophies, theories, models, and types of leaders defined.

I once considered myself an expert on some of my favorite subjects, leadership being one of them. Now I consider myself only a student, and learning continually as much as I can. After studying different books and articles on leadership, I can tell you there are many common schools of thought. There are also many thoughts that, while different and varied, originate from similar (if not the same) philosophies. I can also tell you, the insight that Michael offers us is not so common. His approach and topic choices are as unique as his background. You won't find another author dig into these matters the way he does.

I have known Michael for 15 years in multiple leadership roles from label President, College Professor, Worship Pastor, and other notable positions. Michael's life in leadership has been shaped by his education, being an educator, as an executive, entrepreneur, consultant, working musician, producer, being in management, in ministry, as a father, husband, son, brother, mentor, servant, respected industry leader, Christian, who is also a disciplined, discipled, dedicated & humble follower, when necessary. In those leadership roles, I saw Michael, watched him, and learned from him as a LEADER.

Being in a leadership role and being a leader are two different things. The leadership title has been glorified and glamorized. Leadership is not a title or position. Leadership is not entitlement or self-appointed privilege. Leadership is not determined by age or gender. Leadership is not about time or tenure. Leadership is about influence, inspiration, sacrifice, care, vision, significance, responsibility, motivating, and being willing to serve. A leader exhibits those qualities while also possessing wisdom, clarity, insight, passion, integrity, intelligence, and honesty.

Note-taking is recording or capturing information from another source. I am a note-taker. I have notes on my phone, and I still write notes of some fashion daily.

Not to mention the notes I jot down while reading books, from that "good" sermon, or when I hear something said that's worth repeating! Notes are a way to remind me to review something that I need to rewind (go back to), recall (use later), or remember (hold onto).

What I love most about the very concept of "notes," is that it implies study. As a leader, you should commit to becoming a life-long learner of whatever industry, organization, company, or culture you're a part of.

It is one thing to deduct what you can glean through observation, but it's another to learn when you are getting the exact information first hand from the source. I am excited about us having this information to study, as a resource. I am even happier that Michael was bold enough and courageous enough to use some of the difficulties, the hurts, the issues, and the challenges to expound upon. These chapters could have been picture perfect! Painting and providing anecdotes from a purview that was only about the good, fuzzy occurrences. There are beautiful moments that happen as a leader, but no one prepares you for the ugly ones! This is preparation you will need.

Leadership is fluid. As you grow and/or learn, your leadership style may change...or the need to adapt to a change in business or an ever-changing business climate may present itself. Having to make hard decisions is a part of it, but what happens when you have to lead when hard things are happening to you or done to you? Leading is as much about loving, and loving isn't always easy... especially when the business isn't.

The sum of most of our business amounts to products and people. When leading people, you must identify purpose and also identify problems.

If we consider anything that relates to people, connects to people, needs people to run, used by people, products benefitting people...involving people at any level or any capacity, there is potential for problems. This leadership book addresses some of those problems in a practical, honest, and caring way.

Leadership is not about knowing it all, but retaining as much as your capacity can hold and needs to be successful, according to how you define that success. As you define your success, your leadership style, and your needs...as you overcome your obstacles, achieve goals, and create other leaders, keep these lessons and notes close, and refer to them often.

The words you'll find written are not to only evoke conversation but provide answers, action, inspiration, motivation, application, education, activations, hope and strength for artists, musicians, entrepreneurs, executives, producers, writers, educators, as well as those in ministry and leadership in any arena.

Congratulations on being here. Wisdom tells me, if you are reading this sentence, because you have this book...you are or likely are...a leader. The odds are great that you are already inspiring and impacting an audience, tribe, group, company, or ensemble. You have identified yourself as a leader, are currently in a leadership role, or aspire to be one! People who don't have an interest, nor identity wouldn't want the information or have a need for the ideas being presented here. The only thing else to be sure of is your heart. I am a firm believer that many are the plans that you could make, and proven advice can be shared with you from now to forever, but if your heart is not in the right place...you run the risk of it going wrong. This is not about being a perfect person, but rather a leader who strives to make progress.

Michael is an authority, and the gift to us is that he has some real and relevant notes to share, from the roles he has held and the experiences he has lived. This is a process that, if all taken to heart, with a passionate and genuine pursuit, will help us to realize the greatness as leaders, that I believe is in us to become!

Gina Waters Miller
Senior VP/General Manager, Entertainment One

I met Pastor Michael Weatherspoon when I took a position at a rapidly growing church where he was Pastor of Worship, and I was the director of volunteers. It quickly became apparent to me that in addition to his tremendous gift for music and music production, Pastor Weatherspoon had a gift for people. I had over 20 years of experience building and leading teams, but this was my first official pastoral assignment. It was the first time people were calling me "Pastor Pam," and I wanted to do well. Pastor Weatherspoon's ability to understand, empathize, and connect with those in his department became a standard for me.

For most of us, our emotional intelligence (EQ) will play a larger factor in attaining personal and professional success than our IQ ever will. Every leader is in the people business. Whether you are in the C-suite of a Fortune 500 Company or the assistant coach of a soccer team of eight-year-olds, you will rise or fall based on your ability to lead people wisely. That type of wisdom is found in perspective.

The greatest change any organization can make is in the place of leadership. The greatest change any leader can make is in the place of perspective. I count it a gift whenever I get to say, "I never saw it that way!" Every time I enter a meeting, church, or business, I pray, "Show me what's below the surface." I crave those "aha" moments. They increase my wisdom and expand my world.

If you've ever wished there was a help desk for leaders, your wish has been granted. In *Notes to a Leader*, Pastor Michael Weatherspoon has compiled the answers to the challenges faced by leaders from every sector of society. As you read, take note of the principles taught and how they apply to your world. As the song says, "People make the world go 'round." Great leaders keep it from spinning out of control.

#LeadbetterFollowbetter,

Dr. Pam Ross
Trainer, Consultant, and Author of *Serving, Leading and Loving, a survival guide for Kingdom leaders* and *The Force of JOY, building an unstoppable you*

introduction

"A leader...is like a shepherd. He stays behind the flock, letting the most nimble go out ahead, whereupon the others follow, not realizing that all along they are being directed from behind."

The Long Walk to Freedom

Shepherd leadership is a matter of selfless service to subordinates. This service to others will require a commitment to serve without the potential of immediate recognition or reward. Shepherd leadership will require leaders to gently lead those in their charge — mentoring and teaching them along the way.

So...are you a shepherd who is really a leader? Or, are you a leader who operates as a shepherd? You will be surprised to know that if you are one, you really should be the other. You do not have to be a senior pastor of a church to be a shepherd. In fact, the majority of shepherd leaders have nothing to do with religion. Military officials, coaches, CEOs, management, general managers of sports teams, teachers, academic advisors, Girl Scout leaders, mentors, etc. are, in fact, shepherds as well.

If people have been put in your care and you are responsible for their growth, well-being, and guidance, by default, you are a shepherd — whether you are religious or not. Now, whether you are actually operating as a shepherd leader is another question altogether.

Many people believe that what makes you have a "shepherd's heart" is simply that you care. But that is only half of the equation. What makes you have the true heart of a shepherd is that you have **TIME** for those you lead. That is the other half of the equation. In addition to nurturing and caring for them, **TIME** is needed. **TIME** makes you available and accessible and allows you to know when something is wrong or when they have gone astray. **CARE** needs **TIME** to activate it. If you don't have **TIME**, **CARE** is useless.

Throughout my lifetime, I've learned that there are many types of amazing shepherd leaders. There are:

The Scholar
Leaders who enjoy scholarly debates and stay on top of current resources on ideology/theology.

The Caregiver
Leaders who take care of the people they are responsible for. These leaders seldom miss a need.

The Evangelist
The mission of the organization or entity almost "oozes" out of these leaders. Few people they meet don't hear some

part of good news from The Evangelist. These leaders are always preaching the mission of the organization, company, association, fraternity, etc.

The Entrepreneur
Leaders who love dreaming new ways to grow and support the organization.

The Leader's Leader
Those who continually read works on leadership and being "the best leader" possible are critical to their mission.

The Counselor
Leaders who enjoy one-on-one counseling sessions. Dealing with the problems of the people they lead doesn't drain them.

The Team Builder
Building their team of staff, lay leaders, members, employees, players, etc., takes up much of their time — by choice. And, as a consequence of this, their team tends to serve loyally and long-term.

The Maintenance Man
These leaders enjoy the day-to-day maintenance of the people they lead. Daily calls, emails, check-ins, and drop-ins are their norm, and they enjoy doing these kinds of tasks.

The Wise Leader

Leaders who understand that the organization and culture need to hear the voice of an oracle, and are unafraid to be that voice. They seldom, if ever, avoid a tough issue.

The Developer

These leaders regularly invest in young leaders, guiding them toward growth and challenging them. Likely, several members they have invested in are now doing what they do.

The Community Shepherd

They lead in their organizations and the community. These leaders are the big bro/sis or aunt/uncle of the community. They can be found at the Boys and Girls Club weekly, as children and families love to talk with them about their personal issues. They are known for mediating with gangs, police, and government officials. They are usually well-known and trusted community activists.

Naturally, I've also learned that there are shepherd leaders whose personal issues hinder their ability to lead. They are:

The Emotionally Sick Leader

These leaders are fatigued and depressed. Emotional health is usually not a priority because, in their minds, their heavy workload doesn't allow time for self-renewal and introspection.

The Overly-Driven Leader

Typically, they are in overdrive because they have something to prove to themselves and others. Sometimes, these leaders do not lead with a pure heart. Their leadership is driven by competition and an innate need for success. The number of followers, mentees, and members they have inflate...or deflate their sense of self-worth.

The Fleshly Leader

These are leaders who never fully dealt with their issues, emotions, and wounds before assuming a position of influence. They develop unhealthy lifestyles as a coping mechanism to deal with stress and/or emotional pain. For this leader, more success, influence, and popularity present more temptation. As they climb the ladder, they gain more opportunities to engage in immoral behavior due to the mutual carnal desires between themselves and subordinates who are enamored with them.

The Faddish Leader

These leaders are always attending conferences, reading books, and talking to successful leaders to discover "the next new thing." They lead based on fads and experience high turnovers in who they mentor or lead. Those who follow them eventually grow tired of their unstable leadership style and leave in search of a more stable leader.

The Bitter Leader

These leaders have undealt with anger, bitterness, and unforgiveness from past wounds that were either self-inflicted or the result of real betrayal. Instead of taking responsibility for their failures, they justify their lack of success by continually shifting blame towards others. They are always fighting something and someone and always seem to be a victim. The Bitter Leader tends to blackball those who won't stick with them and speak badly about anyone who doesn't agree with them.

The Superstar

They always have an entourage surrounding them. It's difficult for people who could benefit from the knowledge and expertise they possess to connect with them. These leaders are generally superficial with the people they lead and prefer one-sided relationships. They talk to subordinates as if they have the most important leader in the world, and they constantly want to be honored, served, esteemed, and acknowledged.

The Professional

These kinds of leaders have no real passion for those who follow them. They view their leadership as a mere job and/ or profession. They clock in and clock out. Everything they do is for "sale" and has a price. These are the "hirelings" Jesus spoke about (John 10) who run when the wolves come to devour the sheep because they are not true shepherds but mere professionals. Leadership is all about business for them.

The Compromising Leader
These leaders are passive-aggressive and have a hard time making decisions. They don't want any problems, issues, or controversy. They are typically good-hearted individuals. The Compromising Leader steers clear of ruffling anyone's feathers.

The Legalist
This is the kind of leader who weighs subordinates down with rules, traditions, and regulations. They lack grace, have unreasonable standards, and place heavy burdens on those who follow them. These leaders make serving difficult, as it is often impossible to please them. Those who follow them often feel inadequate, anxious, and afraid.

The Progressive Leader
These leaders are always on the cutting edge of culture and technology. They often mishandle the people they deal with and can care less about how people feel when it is time to "move." While this is usually a good thing, sometimes, this kind of leader does away with the old for the sake of the new... even when the old works best. Though these leaders could benefit from having more seasoned leaders in their lives, they prefer to keep company with other progressive leaders.

The Traditionalist
This leader is the protector and maintainer of the old ways of doing things, whether they are effective today or not.

The Island
The Island Leader has no deep relationships and tries to work out every situation on their own. They isolate themselves and are always suspicious of the true intent and motives of others. They do not work well with other leaders, and they tend to make decisions without seeing the full picture, which results in unwise decision making.

The Independent Leader
This is the alpha leader who thinks they have the best ideas, the most knowledge, and are not always open to having peer-based accountability. They are not a functional part of an association or network of leaders. They can be unreasonably picky in who they lead.

The Mystic
Mystic leaders lack the ability to be practical with life applications when those that follow them need it. Their thoughts and responses are always ethereal but not always applicable.

The Analyst
This leader depends heavily on their intellect and is overly

systematic in how they lead. They are usually know-it-alls and don't ask the intrusive questions to those they lead to help them make objective decisions and provide sound advice.

As you read the descriptions, maybe you found yourself in one or more of these types of leaders. Whether good or bad, you identify as a leader and, therefore, are in need of the wisdom shared in this book.

Our life experiences shape who we are and who we are dictates how we lead. Leading well requires a lot of intentional time working on the issues that have affected us. There are countless books that instruct leaders on how to build, empower, nurture, motivate, inspire, and develop those they lead. However, there are few books available to help leaders deal with issues that impact them as a person.

In a time when leaders can't appear to be vulnerable or must show themselves as invincible, many need resources to help them effectively resolve what ails them. The truth is, no matter how rich, powerful, influential, or popular you are, life affects you just as it affects those you lead. Think about it. How do you address the issues of life that could cause you to give up, throw in the towel, walk away, or simply disappear on those you are responsible for? While you are investing all or the majority of your time dealing with issues that come up in the lives of those you lead, who is helping you address yours? Where do you go for a quick pick-me-up or just a push to keep going?

Regardless of which type of leader you identified with, this book is designed to be to you what you strive daily to be to others. As you dive into *Notes to a Leader*, you will find that this book is a companion when the world refuses to comprehend; an encouraging wake-up call when reality seems challenging to face; a refreshing wind when giving up appears to be the best option; clarity in the midst of fogginess; and wisdom you need for the journey ahead.

"...As we let our own light shine, we unconsciously give other people permission to do the same. As we are liberated from our own fear, our presence automatically liberates others."
Marianne Williamson

note one:

chosen

written to the leader who looks at their place in line.

"Everyone cannot elevate or even revelate at the same time and/or season; an appointment to elevation can result from being specially chosen...like fruit that is ready, ripe and refined for its pleasurable taste."

Tracey Bond

In 2000, Michael Jordan, then the President of the Washington Wizards, needed to hire a head coach. Jordan's first choice was Mike Jarvis, the coach at St. John's University in New York. However, they could not agree on financial terms. Jordan then called Leonard Hamilton. Hamilton agreed to take the position and signed a five year, ten-million-dollar contract. At the press conference, a reporter asked Hamilton how he felt about NOT being the initial choice of Michael Jordan, and his response was, "I was my wife's second choice, and we've been married almost 31 years, and I'm happy with that position." He is still married to her today and now a very successful coach at Florida State University. Don't miss this: He was not his wife's second marriage...he was her second choice!

Leader, do not be concerned about WHERE you are chosen, only that you WERE chosen. When the prophet Samuel was sent to the house of Jessie to find the next king, he went through seven sons BEFORE he got to David. And even then, David's father had to be reminded about him by Samuel asking, "Is there yet another?" In addition to being overlooked by his father, David had to wait before he started the job. He was anointed king as a teenager but did not take the position until he was 30. David could have sulked at the fact that his seven older brothers were held in higher regard to become the king. He could have become angry that his father didn't remember him. He could have even thought that he was too young, and his physical statue did not meet that of a king. He could have grown impatient with waiting to become king. However, he did not concern himself with those things. As a result, he was able to accomplish what no other king before or after him could achieve. He established the walled city of Jerusalem as the capital of his kingdom; he succeeded in subduing all of the surrounding nations plus the entire territory of Israel, and he brought the Ark of the Covenant to Jerusalem.

Once you are selected for leadership, make the best of it. Do not spend time being concerned about when you were interviewed, who else was considered, why it took so long, or how you measure up to others. It is immaterial. You may never be the first call or the best qualified. You may have to watch someone else less skilled and experienced lead as you wait your turn. You may get the call at the last minute, or someone may even be hesitant to call you. But do not concern yourself with that. Many of us are too preoccupied with who was in line ahead of us. Take the leadership position by the horns and never make them regret that they chose you instead of someone else.

As a music industry professional, I was not always the first musician choice by an artist or for studio or live recordings. Most times, I knew that...but it didn't matter. I knew that once I got to rehearsal, the concert, or recording and sat down on those drums or took the headsets to begin to orchestrate, I would make them regret they wasted time calling or considering someone else.

Leaders, once you are selected, whatever the position, function, or responsibility, do not concern yourself with WHERE you were chosen...only THAT you were chosen!

"It is quite rare for God to provide a great man at the necessary moment to carry out some great deep, which is why when this unusual combination of circumstance does occur, history at once records the name of the chosen one and recommends him to the admiration of posterity."
Alexandre Dumas

note two:

offended

written to the leader who has been mishandled.

"The person who offends and the person who has been offended and awaiting for revenge has one thing in common: the real uncertainties of tomorrow are truly uncertain to both of them."

Ernest Agyemang Yeboah

Being offended (due to being wronged) and a spirit of offense (entitlement, pride, and control) are not the same. To suggest that they are is like saying someone who has a drink is a drunk. Although alcohol is the common denominator in both, it does not make you the latter.

You will not go through life without offending or being offended by someone. It is inevitable and unavoidable even if it is not intentional.

The word offense is a translation of the Greek word *skandalizo* (verb) and *skandalon* (noun), which means *a trap or snare; any impediment placed in the way and causing one to stumble or fall* (which can be an act, deed or word). *Skandalizo* and *skandalon* are where we get the English word, *scandal*, which means a *discrediting caused by irreligious conduct*. Leaders should never become captivated by scandal. Scandal blurs your focus and causes your eyes to wander left and right. It slows your stride and causes you to take longer to get to your desired destination. Additionally, scandal keeps you in idol conversation, unsubstantiated claims, and innuendo.

Avoid it at all costs.

The phrase "a spirit of offense" is not found in the Bible. Offenses are caused by (1) The incorrect interpretation of an item or (2) the conduct of one person towards another. What may start off as offense, if left untreated due to mishandling, may become a "spirit" that dictates, drives, and directs your life. This offense creates narratives to the offended. When there is relationship, narratives (whether true or false) are oftentimes created by an action. When there is no relationship, a narrative can always be imagined.

Let's quickly look at key indicators to conclude when someone has a spirit of offense:

1. **Entitlement:** Feeling that one is owed something. Typically, something that was never discussed.

2. **Pride:** Self-reliant instead of God reliant.

3. **Unfairness:** Belief that one has been treated unfairly even when handled properly.

4. **Respect:** A need to demand the respect one feels is due.

5. **Control:** A need to control situations to produce the outcome one desires.

Before we discuss the person who is offended, we must look at offense from a leadership perspective.

Unfortunately, many leaders project offense on subordinates to avoid dealing with issues that WE have created. Why? Because we don't want to be accountable for how we have handled people and the decisions we have made. Leaders have an obligation to ensure that people, places, and things are handled correctly. It won't keep people from becoming offended, but it will keep the offense from being originated by a lack of mismanagement.

For the subordinate, you may have the right to be offended by what was done to you, but you can't let it turn into a spirit that will control you. Offense, when not properly addressed, is like a cancer. It will eat away at you. You will create narratives that are not true, see enemies that do not exist, and distance allies who are vital to your purpose and success.

The spirit of Absalom is simply unresolved issues and this is oftentimes the key cog when dealing with offense. In many instances, offense takes place when issues have not been properly resolved between two or more parties. In 2 Samuel 13, if King David had dealt with the rape of his daughter when he was told about it, Absalom would have never become offended and rose up against him.

Here is what many people miss when the topic of offense comes up: Offense can be justified. Absalom was correct in his offense, but wrong in how he responded. Absalom was initially offended by the mishandling of a situation that the leader (David) should have addressed. This offense caused Absalom to kill his brother Amnon; this offense caused him to sleep with his father's wives and concubines on the rooftop in public to humiliate him; this offense caused him to create an insurrection on his father's kingdom by taking the complaints of people at the temple gates; this offense caused him to set up a coup attempt by galvanizing men that caused his father to flee his own kingdom. Absalom's actions were the result of the offense from an unresolved issue that took root in him.

Good leaders address problems. They understand that conflict resolution wards off a catastrophe; an apology extends a road; a meeting brings forth understanding; a phone call soothes a seething heart; addressing matters keeps the mind from coming to its own conclusions.

Leaders, we can no longer simply tell people to get over it, ignore it, or even send someone else to address it. Deal with the offense before the offense deals with you.

"You may not be able to do anything about how you feel; but you can do something about how you act. People will definitely offend you willing or unwilling by their words and actions... but you can choose to let that offence sink you down or not...."
Israelmore Ayivor

note three:

persistence

written to the leader who is ready to walk away.

*"Nothing in this world can take the place of persistence.
Talent will not: nothing is more common than unsuccessful
men with talent. Genius will not; unrewarded genius is almost
a proverb. Education will not: the world is full of educated
derelicts. Persistence and determination alone are omnipotent."*
                                                    Calvin Coolidge

Setting goals with deadlines usually causes us to work harder to meet expectations such as weight loss, marriage, degree completion, childbearing, improved finances, etc. Unfortunately, when deadlines arrive, and goals are unmet, instead of pressing forward with vigor, we become discouraged, and our persistence is deflated.

In addition to unmet expectations, comparison also kills persistence. Have you ever noticed why horses running in races or pulling wagons wear blinders? Horses wear blinders to prevent them from becoming distracted or panicked by their surroundings. Blinders block the side views of the horse, forcing it to only look forward. The problem with many of us is that as we work on our goals, instead of looking at what is before us, we spend a lot of time checking out what's going on to our left and right. We gauge the success of our pace by what others present on social media, at work or school, and in church or the industry. We fail to realize that much of what we see on social media is pure imagery that must be maintained and may lack accuracy. Additionally, we forget that though people may work with us, attend the same church or school, or be in the same industry, their story is different from ours. The journey that led to where they are now may have been long, tedious, treacherous, and filled with many obstacles and perils.

You will find no greater area to look for stories of persistence than in the music industry. Many artists have been touring, singing, playing, and writing for years with no to minimal success — but they have kept going. One of my favorite examples of persistence is the gospel artist and songwriter, Vashawn Mitchell.

I've known Vashawn Mitchell since he was a teenager. Growing up in the same city, Harvey, Illinois, I encountered his talent while playing for choirs he directed on several occasions, such as Thornton High School Gospel Choir and St. Mark Missionary Baptist Church. As an adult, Vashawn moved to Sweet Holy Spirit Church in Chicago and worked even harder to establish himself as a prolific songwriter, producer, and director. The ministry recorded several albums under his direction.

In 2010, Vashawn released an album called *Triumphant*. It was a success due to a song on the album entitled, "Nobody Greater." This album catapulted Vashawn to the top. This song brought him 11 Stellar Awards nominations and several Dove Award nominations. "Nobody Greater" was the most popular gospel song in America for 2011 and 2012 and probably beyond. Every church in America was singing this song.

In 2015, I was asked to speak at a music conference. My audience was young up-and-coming artists who needed encouragement and perspective. Before the conference, I called Vashawn and asked him, "How many albums did you do before you released *Triumphant*?"

He thought for a moment and said, "Seven. I did four with Sweet Holy Spirit, and three on my own."

I thought to myself, Wow. Seven albums. Though Vashawn wrote many songs, had many rehearsals, and did many shows, he didn't get to the top until album number eight. What if he had quit at album number five? What if he threw in the towel at album six? What if he got discouraged and walked away even earlier and stopped at album three? He wouldn't be reaping the benefits now. Because he remained persistent, he was able to reach the success his talent merited.

I shared this story at the conference, and I told the audience of new artists that if you believe in what you do and who you are, stay persistent. Your success is not going to happen because you release music, it may not happen at the time you have predetermined, it may not happen at the moment you've spent all your money touring and singing in venues where no one shows up, but if you stay persistent, in time, you will eventually be revealed to an audience that will propel you to success. Don't look at what others are doing. Refrain from doing what is popular. Stay true to who you are, and don't compare your journey to others.

Leaders, it may take a little longer than expected. You may feel frustrated. You may want to hand the assignment off to someone else or abandon it altogether. You may spend all your money, put great effort into ideas that no one supports, and give your all, but still not see the desired results. Nevertheless, if you feel you have been called to this, remain diligent. Success may not happen when you feel it should, you must remain persistent.

"To make our way, we must have firm resolve, persistence, tenacity. We must gear ourselves to work hard all the way. We can never let up."

Ralph Bunche

note four:

desperation

written to the leader struggling with doing it alone.

"Desperation is sometimes as powerful an inspirer as genius."

Benjamin Disraeli

I n 1970, Paramount Pictures was running out of money and American Zoetrope Film Company, formed by Francis Ford Coppola and George Lucas, was completely out of money from the release of a failed film called, "THX 1138." Peter Bart, the VP of Paramount, the fifth oldest surviving film studio in the world and the second oldest in the United States, came up with a brilliant idea. He thought, "Let's purchase the rights to commercial novels and make movies from adapted screenplays and pitch them to young, up and coming directors to film them." (Instead of continuing with the old model of using experienced directors who are creating original screenplays. An original screenplay is a movie not based on previously published material. An adapted screenplay is a movie created from published material, like comic books, novels, journals, etc.)

Paramount purchased the rights to "The Godfather" and pitched it to Coppola, but he turned it down several times. Bart, in a last attempt, met with Coppola and told him, "You are broke, and we have very little money left. You need to do this film." Coppola relented and eventually accepted. The movie went on to gross the most money all-time (up to that point) since "Gone with the

Wind" in 1939. "The Godfather" is considered to be the best movie of all-time by many film critics. Because of this collaboration, Star Wars, Return of the Jedi, Apocalypse Now, Indiana Jones, and many other prominent films came forth. Coppola has directed 22 films since then, and Lucas has 35 to his credit.

What is the point? Sometimes your success is going to come when you collaborate with someone who is brilliant...but desperate!

Many are anxious to connect with those who are already a success. Most of the time, those successful individuals will use you and drop you off when they are done. Do not despise joining forces with the desperate. Desperation is fuel to a rocket. There is power in it. Your prosperity may be connected to someone who has no money in their pocket, but a million dollars' worth of brilliance and desperation.

Your breakthrough may be sitting in your email/text inbox, Instagram DMs, or Facebook Messenger. It may be a contact you haven't called back who has been trying to schedule a meeting with you or someone simply wanting to shake your hand after a meeting or presentation. Do not overlook the unassuming, there is opulence there. Everyone is attracted to the obvious, but few see what's in the shadows.

Many of your ideas have not gotten off the ground because you won't merge. You have put yourself on an island. You won't seek assistance. You want to do it all yourself. You are working on assignments that you have limited knowledge of. You are masterful yet secluded. You are looking, but your gaze is too narrow. You are focused but too fixed on the initiative.

Leaders are able to fuse brilliance with desperation from those they lead and manufacture wealth, ideas, resources, solutions, and unsurpassed creativity.

"Many ideas grow better when transplanted into another mind than the one where they sprang up."

Oliver Wendell Holmes

note five:

over-thinking

Written to the leader who has become a prisoner of being analytical.

"Don't get too deep, it leads to over-thinking, and over thinking leads to problems that doesn't even exist in the first place."

Jayson Engay

Thinking analytically is an asset. And it is not as common as people think. Many leaders don't have the ability of a truly analytical mind. It allows you to make objective decisions, be systematic, see detail, solve multiple problems simultaneously, and arrive at an answer quicker than others. Analytical thinkers are more rational than irrational in their leadership style and are able to inquire before making decisions. In essence, they are more objective than subjective when leading. Being an analytical thinker is what caused Einstein to come up with the Law of Relativity after sitting in his chair for hours on end thinking about mass and spacetime.

Many leaders attribute their success to having a mind that can solve problems quickly. They can evaluate a situation just by observing it and can see potential obstacles and have answers or steer clear of them immediately. These leaders can see paintings in detail and decipher a myriad of colors and themes at once without losing sight of the big picture.

But many times, our biggest asset, can cause our biggest handicap. Many leaders have problems shutting their minds off. Their sleep isn't consistent, and they wake up tired every day. They don't seem to have enough energy. They are exhausted all the time trying to figure out multiple problems, many of which is not even under their jurisdiction. They are worried about people they can't reach; accounts they have no access too and decisions beyond their authority to make.

One of the dangers to over-thinking is that it allows you to be able to see forward, but it keeps you looking back. Those who over-think, tend to walk in unforgiveness, not so much for others, but themselves. You replay past scenarios in your mind, what you could have done differently, and why you made certain mistakes. Holding yourself in contempt about things of the past creates enmity between the present and your future. You see the future, but you can't get there because you are thinking too much about what took place in the past. Even when considering your accomplishments, you wonder, "What took so long? Why didn't I accomplish it faster?"

Over-thinking also causes you to create situations that may not exist. A mind that won't turn off can cause you to believe that your friends are your enemies and cause you to think that their responses or decisions were made to harm you or with you in mind when you never even came up in the discussion. You will write plays and perform them in the theater of your mind with characters in full costume with an audience critiquing the performance.

You are the playwright, director, producer, and actor in your own play.

When I graduated from college, I began investing with a financial services company called Janus. When I did some research on the meaning of this name and where it came from, I discovered that Janus was a roman mythological god whose face was split in half. Half of his face looked forward, and the other half look back. He was considered the god of beginnings and transitions. The company's ideology in investing was that it would use observations from past performances and market fluctuations to be able to determine what stocks and funds would be great to invest in for the future, thus having foresight. And this is how many leaders' minds are — one-half forward and one-half looking back due to over-thinking. You can see far ahead with great distance, you can see beyond the problem because of your profound mind, but you keep looking back as if the past is chasing you. Your relationships suffer, your health suffers, your personal happiness suffers, and you feel like you are running in place because you are. You are sweating, breathing hard, and exhausted, but you haven't moved at all. This is all caused by over-thinking.

Leaders, the other thing that keeps you over-thinking, is that you simply spend too much time alone. Isolation causes your mind to always be in a cycle of processing. Let's take a look at a very important scripture that is used a lot at weddings or when leaders are trying to get teams and departments to understand collaboration. Ecclesiastes 4:9-12 (KJV) says:

"Two are better than one; because they have a good reward for their labour.
For if they fall, the one will lift up his fellow: <u>but woe to him that is alone when he falleth;</u> for he hath not another to help him up.
Again, if two lie together, then they have heat: <u>but how can one be warm alone?</u>
And if one prevail against him, two shall withstand him; and a threefold cord is not quickly broken."

One of the things we miss in this scripture is that it also deals with the dangers of isolation. You need friends, equal companionship, support, encouragement, a helping hand, confidants, and trustworthy men and women in your life so that when your mind wants to overtake you, someone is there to help realign your thoughts and keep your mind from wandering in the wilderness ... and they won't penalize you for it.

A leader contacted me one morning and said, "I prayed for you this morning, Michael. I prayed that God would heal your memory." It's not that I had not forgiven; I just couldn't seem to forget. When I was alone, I kept replaying scenarios in my mind. I kept pondering questions like, "What if I had done this or that? Would the outcome have been different? Why did they do this to me? Why did this happen?" The danger of this is that it can lead to condemnation. When that happens, you begin to beat yourself up, even about things that were not your fault.

Your mind is one of your greatest assets, but don't let it control you or wear you down. Use it as a tool; do not make it a liability.

Here's the ultimate danger with over-thinking: The past is making decisions for you instead of your future.

"We can easily manage if we will only take, each day, the burden appointed to it. But the load will be too heavy for us if we carry yesterday's burden over again today, and then add the burden of the morrow before we are required to bear it."

John Newton

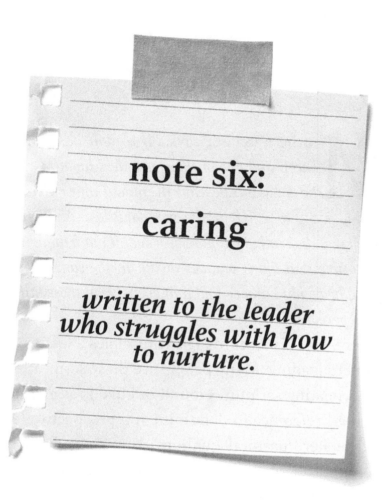

note six:

caring

written to the leader who struggles with how to nurture.

"Leadership is solving problems. The day soldiers stop bringing you their problems is the day you have stopped leading them. They have either lost confidence that you can help or concluded you do not care. Either case is a failure of leadership."

Colin Powell

Matthew 18:12-14 says, *"If a man has a hundred sheep and one of them wanders away, what will he do? Won't he leave the ninety-nine others on the hills and go out to search for the one that is lost? And if he finds it, I tell you the truth, he will rejoice over it more than over the ninety-nine that didn't wander away! In the same way, it is not my heavenly Father's will that even one of these little ones should perish."*

Here, Jesus is teaching His 12 disciples a lesson about shepherd leading. Many people use these scriptures and the correlating scriptures found in Luke 15 as a pastoral/shepherd reference to determine if a prospective leader has shepherd/pastoral qualities. Yes, a shepherd must care. However, these scriptures show us another necessity for leaders that often goes unstated, and that is **TIME**.

CARE caused the shepherd to go after the sheep, but **TIME** caused him to know that the sheep was lost. Your care means nothing if you aren't available. Sheep need shepherds who are available to be in the pasture with them. Your best ability is availability.

Think about being in a relationship. You can profess your love for someone endlessly, but if you are never available to spend time with them, the relationship will be lost. Your significant other will wander right into the arms of someone else

A leader must be available. If you are not around, you won't know that something is wrong before those submitted to you get lost. A leader's willingness to be available can ward off many problems. Nothing good will come out of your people spending considerable amounts of time alone. When leaders don't have time for their posts, the people they are responsible for will eventually wander and become lost.

Years ago, I led a developing music ministry. When I met with the team for the first time, I gave everyone my cellphone number and email. (A number that I answered and an email that I checked daily.) I encouraged them to reach out to me at any time, no matter the issue. I wanted them to know that they had access to me and that I would make myself available to them when they reached out.

After some time, they took me up on my offer, and many individuals on the team began to share their lives with me. It became a norm for them to share their issues, disappointments, triumphs, situations, and circumstances. They would reach out to me for prayer and my blessing in their endeavors; advice on issues with their children, ex-spouses, and parents; and suggestions on who to date or where to go to college. They would contact me to let me know if they were sick, lost a loved one, and sometimes, they just reached out to vent. There was probably nothing that came up that I didn't address, and they appreciated this.

Many of them had no one in their lives who was available. Yes, many of them had people who said they cared, but they didn't have the time. In addition to answering their calls, emails, and texts, I made time to reach out to them. I didn't wait for an issue to arise to engage with my team.

Because I made time for them, they grew closer to me and respected me as their leader. As a result, people developed personally and in their gifts, the team gained confidence and built strong relationships, and the music department became healthy and strong.

Leader, one of the BEST things you can do for those who report directly to you, is returning their calls, emails, texts, and video messages. Sometimes, those you lead know you can't solve their problem. They just need to know you have time to care about it. Simply responding when they reach for you can stop suicide or prevent someone from getting hurt, making a bad decision, failing into addiction, or revisiting bad habits. This kind gesture can even be the turning point for someone on the borderline between disappointment and depression.

For leaders who oversee large teams, it may be impossible or unwise for you to give out your phone number or block out time for individual meetings. Simple gestures such as sending out cards on birthdays and anniversaries, sending encouraging emails and memos, providing comp time and sick leave, allowing parents time to attend their children's events, or encouraging them to take time for self-care, shows those you are responsible for that you care about them as individuals. Don't allow yourself to be so busy for the sake of being busy that you lose the art of being available.

Make yourself available. It will only strengthen the message you are trying to get them to hear.

"If you are capable, but not available, nature will raise a person with lesser ability to replace you soon."

Israelmore Ayivor

note seven:

healing anonymously

written to the leader who can't seem to find a cure for what ails them.

"Do not look for healing at the feet of those who broke you."
Rupi Kaur, Milk and Honey

It's possible you are not healing because where you seek treatment and where you were afflicted...are the same place. It's not that you don't want to heal — you just can't recover in the same place where people want to see you dead. You must remember that an infirmary never gives poison then prescribes a remedy.

For some issues in life, you must go to a neutral place that doesn't care about your title or position, haven't heard a narrative, haven't formed an opinion, and don't know who you are, how much money you make, or who you are connected to. You need a place that only cares about how to help you heal.

You also have to remember that there are some life issues and circumstances that can be remedied from **advice**, such as what college or university to apply too; what companies to seek employment; what neighborhoods are best to live in; or, what school districts are best for your children to attend. However, there are other life issues that require more than advice; they require **counsel**, such as separation, divorce, anxiety, rape, incest, addiction, etc. If you seek healing in the same location you experienced the trauma, you may not find it. Why? Because not everyone at that location where the trauma took place is capable of handling issues to bring you towards healing.

When we are in need of healing, we often look for the person who is positioned, held in high regard, or in leadership. However, just because someone has a title does not mean they have the maturity required to help you heal or the ability to separate the trauma or infraction from who YOU are and what you can become.

Let's take a look at the differences between advice and counsel/counseling. **Advice** is a relevant piece of information (a point of view or opinion offered) given by a superior, confidant, mentor, or advisor, to resolve a problem, provide a solution, or overcome difficulty. This is often known as guidance, and it can be received or ignored by the person requesting advice. Advice may or may not be of any significance.

Counsel/counseling refers to professional advice given by a **counselor** to an individual to help him in overcoming academic, personal, life, or psychological problems. Counseling is the process by which a counselor identifies the root cause of a problem, and the counselee solves it by acting upon the decision arrived. All counsel is advice, but not all advice is counsel. What makes this distinction? Who you seek advice and counsel from. Not everyone is a counselor, but anyone can give you advice. The only thing advice requires is an opinion.

Counselors make objective decisions and not subjective. Counselors are not influenced by personal feelings or opinions in considering and representing facts. They do not let their emotions get in the way. They remain objective and limit the ability for subjectivity to guide the outcome. They know how to separate YOU from the ISSUE. And if they have to choose a side, they side with what is RIGHT.

The other aspect of counsel/counseling is **confidentiality**. Proverbs 11:13-14 reads, *"A talebearer revealeth secrets: but he that is of a faithful spirit concealeth the matter. Where no counsel is, the people fall: but in the multitude of counsellors there is safety."*

We often goes to this scripture and go directly to verse 14. But we often overlook verse 13 and the discussion of talebearing. Talebearing means, *"a person who maliciously gossips and reveals secrets."* Counselors do not gossip or reveal secrets. The easiest way to determine if who you want to share your issues with or who represents themselves as a counselor or confidant is worthy of it is to listen to how much they repeat issues about others. If you hear about issues on others from them, others will hear about issues from them on you. They are not counsel... even with a title.

It's harder to reconcile a thing once you've opened it up to public scrutiny. A hospital does not announce its patients. Nor does a doctor publish what he's prescribed. You may not be healing because what you thought you shared with a "confidant" has been released for public consumption. Public opinion is like termites in wood. The outside looks pristine until you crack the wood open and see all the internal damage. As you attempt to hold it together and look good on the outside until you get through the process of your trauma or dilemma, your inner man has ceased to heal because the public has become aware of something that should have been kept. A counselor holds your information in confidence and lets you decide what and when information is disseminated. Counselors are confidants. They do not expose, tarnish, or defame you. They seek healing.

Even though someone may have a title, they may not possess the ability to remain confidential. Remember this:

<u>Counsel/Counselors...</u>

- are not the cause of your trauma.
- see you as who you are and not what you did or what happened.
- are objective.
- are confidential.
- will keep you anonymous.

Leaders, sometimes, your healing is dependent on your anonymity.

"We were alone together for three days, we knew no one in the city, I could be anyone, say anything, do anything. I felt like a war prisoner who's suddenly been released by an invading army and told that he can start heading home now, no forms to fill out, no debriefing, no questions asked, no buses, no gate passes, no clean clothes to stand in line for — just start walking."
André Aciman, Call Me by Your Name

note eight:

trauma

written to the leader who struggles with letting go of the experience.

"After all, when a stone is dropped into a pond, the water continues quivering even after the stone has sunk to the bottom."
Arthur Golden, Memoirs of a Geisha

Trauma is defined by Webster's Dictionary as, "a deeply distressing or disturbing experience." I graduated from Gwendolyn Brooks Junior High School in Harvey, Illinois. I was an eighth-grade graduate, ready to embark upon high school. During the summer before my freshman year, a letter came in the mail from Thornridge High School. It was from the head coach of the football team about try-outs and summer conditioning. I was so excited to get this letter, as I had always dreamed of being a football player. I had a football player trading card collection that had hundreds, if not a thousand players. I always dreamed of being a running back on the football team. I was fast, light on my feet, and quick as lightning.

I asked my mom if I could try out, and she allowed me to do so. I went to summer camp, and it was pretty hard. We trained in 90 plus degree weather for summer conditioning with our football coach, Mr. Lunak. He was cut from the old (South Eastern Conference) SEC mold. As if he was with Coach Bear Bryant and the Junction City Boys who went through the grueling camp down in Texas in 1954.

After summer camp, I made the freshman team. I was a lightweight. I may have been 140 pounds and 5'11", but I sure was shifty and fast. I became the starting running back for the B-team. The A-team's starting running back was Tyrone Washington. He was built like Eric Dickerson. Physically, he was more suited for the A-team.

Our season began with a game against Richards High School, and I did very well. I was excited. I felt good about my performance in the opening game. Our second game of the season was against Shephard High School. It was an away game, and we were on their campus. In the 3rd quarter, we were up by a touchdown, and the quarterback in the huddle called the play, "Right 47 sweep, on 2!" The play was a sweep to me that bounced off the Left Tackle.

We went to the line, and the center hiked the ball on the second count. The quarterback tossed the ball to me, I bounced off the Left Tackle, and saw an opening. Five yards, ten yards... I dodged the linebackers and was into the secondary. I made a move to the sideline and was about to spin off the cornerback when I was suddenly hit in the back by a big linebacker and was driven into the ground. A cry came out of my mouth that must have rung throughout the city. I was carried off the field holding my wrist.

My wrist swelled up, and I knew it was broken. I couldn't move it. I was taken to the ER later that evening, but they could not put a cast on it. I had to wait three days to see a specialist. So for the weekend, I was in excruciating pain.

On Tuesday, I saw a specialist who had examined the x-rays. I was lying on the patient's bed when he came in, looked at my wrist, and walked out of the room. Suddenly, two large men entered the room. One held my upper body down, and the other grabbed my legs. The specialist walked back in, grabbed my arm, and bent my wrist. Yes... the wrist that was broken. I screamed, twisted, and tried to break free, but I couldn't. I was being held down by two large men, and the doctor had my arm.

After everything settled down, I asked the doctor why he did that to me. He replied that my elbow was out of place, and in order to get my elbow back in place, he had to reset my wrist so that it would heal in alignment.

It took three months to heal. The pain of the injury was one thing, but the experience in the doctor's office left a memory that I will never forget.

In October of the same year, basketball try-outs began. Of course, I wanted to play on the basketball team. Not only did I love playing football, I loved playing basketball also. Games of "21", backyard and playground ball, and the trusty hanger in the door with socks and roundup tape as your ball were the norm. I wanted to try out for the team, but I still was wearing a split. I had not played in months.

I tried out anyway, and made the team with a splint on

my wrist and having not been in the best of shape. I had a great year playing on the team at the shooting guard and small forward position. I stayed on the team, and in subsequent years, ran indoor track.

Every year, from my sophomore year to my senior year, the football coaches asked me if I would come back to the football team. Each time I said no. I never told them why, but for me, the incident was too traumatic. I got over the pain of breaking my wrist, separating my elbow, waiting three days to get a cast. But I never forgot the trauma of being held down by two men as my broken wrist and arm were twisted.

What lesson does this story present for leaders? Just because I experienced trauma in one sport did not mean that sports were not for me. Had I let the traumatic incident stop me, I would have never tried out for other sports, in fear that I would get hurt. Even though basketball is not a contact sport, the risk of injury is still high.

Just because you experienced trauma in a leadership position at one place...does not mean you are not a leader.

My football injury did not cause me to question whether I was a good basketball player and a great runner in the 100 and 200-meter dash. It just confirmed that, even though I was fast, shifty, and quick, at 140 pounds, football was not the best sport for me.

Don't let a trauma from your past cause you not to

in your present. Remember, I am not talking about a wound (physical)...I'm talking about the trauma (experience). My wrist and elbow healed. Though the "experience" remained in my mind, it didn't stop me from sports.

Wounds are the response from trauma.

"You're in shock. You can't afford to be in shock. Two parts of himself were having a conversation. You were probably meant to think of yourself as 'I' when talking to yourself."

Jack Grimwood, Moskva

note nine:

addiction

written to the leader
who has become
enslaved to a bad habit.

"I have absolutely no pleasure in the stimulants in which I sometimes so madly indulge. It has not been in the pursuit of pleasure that I have periled life and reputation and reason. It has been the desperate attempt to escape from torturing memories, from a sense of insupportable loneliness and a dread of some strange impending doom."

Edgar Allan Poe

Earlier this year, I was asked to speak at an international music clinic. I was so excited to get the call. When I received the news, I was actually in Toronto speaking to a group of musicians, singers, and leaders at Canada Christian College. I was honored that one of my favorite singers, who founded the clinic, asked me to be a speaker. I was on the line up with some very well-known speakers, and within a week of being asked, I knew what I was going to talk to the attendees about. It was as if I knew what needed to be said in the room eight months before the clinic event took place. It felt as though the presentation was written specifically for each person in the room.

The clinic started on a Thursday, and creatives from every sector: singers, musicians, music producers, event planners, photographers, social media managers, dancers, songwriters, publicists, and pastors from three continents gathered, ready to learn and worship together.

I presented that Friday afternoon, and I love to use

PowerPoint when I present. As usual, I had more slides than I had time, but I was able to get through a good portion of my content.

That night, Pastor John Hannah preached a powerful message to close the clinic. At the end, he did an altar call for everyone serious about their assignment in music ministry. The entire room bombarded the stage and pulpit area and formed a circle around him. As the people were walking up to the stage, a young man slipped a folded note in my hand. He gave it to me without even looking in my eye, sort of clandestine. It was as if he didn't want anyone seeing him give it to me. I watched him walk on the stage, moved to the side, and opened up the note. It read, "Please pray for me. I am a worship leader, and I'm addicted to pain medication. Thank You."

I stood in shock for a moment and wondered why he gave it to me. Why did he walk past all of those leaders and come directly to me? Was I the leader he was closest to heading to the stage? Was he going to hold onto it, but that last impulse as he went on stage nudged him to give it to me? I mean, I've never been addicted to any medication, drugs, or alcohol. I'm not a recovering addict. Why would I get this note? As quickly as those questions came to mind, they disappeared. It didn't matter. He slipped me a note because he was desperate. He was looking for someone to help him. He was looking for a lifeline, and he or God, chose me at that very moment, and I had to respond.

As the room began to pray, it was a sight to see. A sea of creatives locked arm-in-arm praying for each other. Pastor John Hannah was sincerely praying for people, hugging people, and crying out to God for them as a child cries out for their mother when they need to be fed.

After about five minutes, I went into the pulpit, and in the sea of people, I found him. I told him to lift his hands, and I began to pray for him. I prayed against his addiction and the shame and condemnation that would seek to make him feel like a failure.

After the prayer, I walked off the stage. Pastor John Hannah was still praying, and I had to be in order and let him finish and talk to the entire group of people. I lost visual contact with the singer after the prayer ended and everyone started exiting the stage, as it was several hundred on the stage exiting at one time. I was looking for him afterward to ask if I could stay in contact with him and be some accountability for him. I wanted to let him know that I cared.

That evening, when I got back to my hotel, I pondered on the night. I remembered that in my presentation, I mentioned that as leaders, when we struggle heavily with certain things, whether drugs, sex, alcohol, gambling, porn, etc., it not only affects you or your family, but it also affects the people you lead whether at work, church, entertainment, government, or other areas. Those "dark forces" can seep through the room and latch on to those you are in charge of nurturing. You will find that the struggles that have a stronghold on you will begin to present themselves in people that you care for as a leader.

I explained this clearly in my teaching, and I'm sure it convicted him. But the care in which I presented it gave him the courage to come to me for prayer.

Leaders, we all have issues. We all have struggled with something in our lives. Don't feel shame or condemn yourself. You are digging a hole and standing in it, and the dirt you are shoveling out falls back on your head into the hole. You are not a failure. Ask someone to help you.

As leaders, we are taught to be strong, hide, handle things alone, put on our Sunday's best clothes, be suited and booted, and walk out the door without a care in the world. The reality, for most, is that we carry stuff to our cars, apartments, homes, and man caves that we keep from our friends and loved ones who truly want to help.

I don't know what happened to this young man. I believe that my prayer helped. I hope that he has recovered and surrounded himself with a support team. I hope that he didn't give up being a singer, but took the necessary time to step away so that he can be the best version of him at the mic... and instead of unintentionally releasing the forces of addiction over the microphone. I hope that he can sing a song of redemption and recovery that so many people in these times need from a myriad of issues and circumstances.

"One of the greatest evils is the foolishness of a good man. For the giving man to withhold helping someone in order to first assure personal fortification is not selfish, but to elude needless self-destruction; martyrdom is only practical when the thought is to die, else a good man faces the consequence of digging a hole from which he cannot escape, and truly helps no one in the long run."

Mike Norton, Just Another Love Story

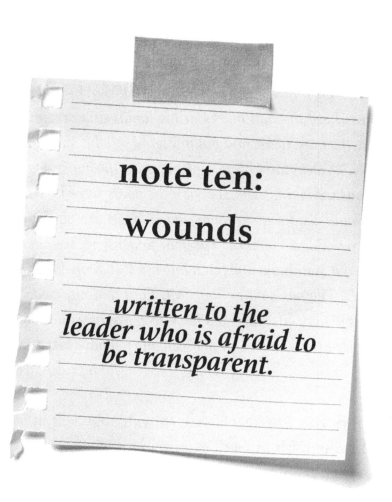

note ten:

wounds

written to the leader who is afraid to be transparent.

"Every wound is a word."

Lailah Gifty Akita

"Now Thomas (also known as Didymus), one of the Twelve, was not with the disciples when Jesus came. So the other disciples told him, "We have seen the Lord!" But he said to them, "Unless I see the nail marks in his hands and put my finger where the nails were, and put my hand into his side, I will not believe." A week later his disciples were in the house again, and Thomas was with them. Though the doors were locked, Jesus came and stood among them and said, "Peace be with you!" Then he said to Thomas, "Put your finger here; see my hands. Reach out your hand and put it into my side. Stop doubting and believe." Thomas said to him, "My Lord and my God!" Then Jesus told him, "Because you have seen me, you have believed; blessed are those who have not seen and yet have believed.""

John 20:24-29 (NIV)

John 20:24-29 teaches us a valuable lesson about having faith in God, even though we can't see Him. When reading these scriptures, one might be in awe of Thomas' lack of faith. I mean, think about it. How could Thomas doubt that Jesus had risen from the dead when he walked with Jesus and saw Him perform countless miracles? How could he doubt a resurrection when Jesus raised three people from the dead when He walked the Earth? He raised the widow's son in the village of Nain.

(Luke 7:15) He raised the 12-year-old daughter of Jairus, a ruler of the synagogue. (Mark 5:42) He raised Lazarus, the brother of Mary and Martha, after Lazarus had been dead four days. (John 11:44) Couldn't the man who raised others from the dead surely raise Himself from the dead? How could you doubt such a thing, Thomas?

As I spent more time exploring this passage, I began to see it from a different perspective — through the lens of Jesus, the leader. By responding to the request of Thomas, Jesus allowed Thomas to see Him in a different light. Would the outcome have been the same if Jesus had appeared and His wounds were not visible? Would Thomas' faith have been increased if Jesus did not allow Thomas to put his finger and hand in His wounds?

When you are willing to show them your wounds, those you lead will become more devoted to your leadership. When you are willing to show them the wound that left a mark, the bruise that still has scar tissue, the cut that was once stitched, or the closed gash that no longer drips blood, their faith in you as their leader won't easily waver. Even more important, they will know that they, too, can survive the difficulties they experience.

Of the 12 disciples, only 1, John the Beloved, witnessed the crucifixion. However, all of Jesus' disciples died tragic deaths. Their faith in Jesus didn't waver when persecution and imminent death were presented to them. Is it possible that Jesus reappearing to them after death and revealing the wounds He suffered from was vital in preparing the apostles for the persecution they would face in the future?

In January 2017, during our beginning-of-the-year meeting, I decided to open up to those who served in the music department I led at the time. Before I discussed the plan for the year, I taught on shame and condemnation, referencing the story in Genesis of Adam and Eve learning that they were naked. In my introduction to the lesson, I talked about a subject that had, for many years prior, caused me to be wounded. As I spoke about my trauma and wounds, I heard someone crying ever so faintly in the back of the church. A couple of people went to console her as I taught. Once the meeting was over, the young lady walked up to me and expressed why she was crying. She had just found out that she was pregnant, and the father of the child abandoned her upon hearing the news. She had been ostracized by some friends, religious people, artists in the music industry, and even her family. She was ashamed and thought that I, the music department, and the church would put her out. I hugged her, told her that we would not abandon her, and affirmed that she was safe with the department and me. I encouraged her not to condemn herself, or be ashamed of others learning of her pregnancy. Just because indiscretions are not showing (in others), it doesn't mean they aren't present (in them). We often condemn people for the indiscretions we can SEE while most people are simply experts at keeping things hidden from public view. I ended by reminding her how much God loved her. She was immediately relieved, and her spirit was revived.

Later that week, many people in the music department shared how their affinity for me grew and how they saw me in a deeper way. My openness about my wounds showed them that I was not just some superstar musician and record producer who was brought in to lead them. Instead, I was, in fact, just like them. Why? Because I showed them my wounds.

Many times, leaders hide behind titles, gifts, and positions, and refuse to allow those who follow to see their wounds. They refuse to let others know that they have been hurt, bruised, torn, and cut. As a result, these leaders appear untouchable and unrelatable. Dear leader, allowing them to see your wounds allows them to touch you. Allowing them to touch you communicates that you are not above them, but you walk alongside them.

Thomas knew that Jesus had been crucified. He knew that Jesus had been buried. Even though his fellow disciples told him that they had seen Jesus, Thomas didn't believe that Jesus overcame the grave until he saw Him. Many times, people will have heard about or even witnessed your persecution, but only the wounds you show will prove to them that you have been revived. Just as Jesus showed Thomas His wounds, so should leaders when the moment calls for it. It can help followers increase their faith. They will know that if their leader overcame it, they can too.

Don't be afraid to remove your clothes and show them the bruises on your body. Even allow them to touch the wound (ask questions). Don't just reveal the wounds caused by the hands of others. Show them the wounds that were self-inflicted as well. This can help those you lead to avoid the pitfalls and bad decision making you made on your journey.

Finally, showing your wounds can ward off idolatry. As leaders, we often only show people our amazing gifts and the side of us that we have perfected. This can cause people to hold you in too high esteem. As a result, when you fall, make a mistake, or are found in error, your relationship with and the faith of those who follow you are impacted negatively. If you never allow them to see your wounds, hear you admit error, watch you apologize, or learn how you corrected your mistakes, they will think that you are perfect. Revealing your wounds will benefit both you and those submitted to your leadership.

Now, there is a word of caution when showing wounds. Leader, you can't show everyone every scar. Use discretion in transparency. People who pressure you to reveal your wounds may be quick to shame you for them and use them as weapons against you at the opportune time. Everyone can't handle every wound you have experienced. Let wisdom guide you on what to share and when. Open wounds that still ooze with blood are not testimonies because you have not overcome them yet. If the wound is still dripping, then selectivity in who sees the wound is key to your recovery. In those situations, be mindful of who you allow to see your wounds.

"Some lessons are best taught, not by others' scars, but by our own wounds."

Mokokoma Mokhonoana

note eleven:
the gifted

written to the leader who over-values talent.

"Imagine if you had baseball cards that showed all the performance stats for your people: batting averages, home runs, errors, ERAs, win/loss records. You could see what they did well and poorly and call on the right people to play the right positions in a very transparent way."

Ray Dalio

B eing gifted does not mean that one has what it takes to be a leader. They are not correlated. If you want people for their gift, then place them in the appropriate gifted position, and they will flourish there.

We have too many leadership positions being filled by gifted people who are ill-equipped to handle the subject matter and the people they are responsible for. Our organizations are floundering for it. While we may be attracted to their performance, enamored by their charisma, mesmerized by their oratory skills, and amazed at their ability to work a room, we must consider if the individual is truly equipped to lead.

There is a difference between a supervisor and a manager. Is it possible that we have placed the gifted in managerial positions even though they do not possess the ability to construct and guide an organization? Have we put the entire future of the organization in the hands of people who cannot assess, set protocol, and steer a ship?

According to the UC Berkley article "Berkley People and Culture", "a manager is responsible for making significant decisions on what the unit does: its purpose, functions and role, and for making commitments and decisions that require the expenditure of significant unit resources. Managers have a significant, external focus (to the world outside the unit)".

A manager is a person responsible for controlling or administering all or part of a company or similar organization. A manager has to perform functions like planning, organizing, staffing, directing, and controlling. These functions are essential for running an organization smoothly and achieving enterprise objectives. Planning is required for setting goals and establishing strategies for coordinating activities. A manager has the ability and skillset to lead a division.

A supervisor is a person in the first-line management who monitors employees in their performance of assigned or delegated tasks. A supervisor's limit on leading people is teams.

A supervisor has a more internal focused responsibility for implementing the manager's decisions through the work of subordinate employees. Once a decision is made on what to do, supervisors have a significant role in deciding how to do it; how to achieve the objective established by the manager. Supervisors often perform the same kind of work that the subordinates do; managers do not do the daily work of the unit as a regular part of their work.

You can be gifted and not fully developed to handle a

position of management and leadership.

To put it plainly...

Keyboardist does not equal an MD (Music Director).
Preacher does not equal a senior pastor.
Recording Artist does not equal a Minister/Pastor of Music
Dancer does not equal a choreographer.
Singer does not equal worship leader.
Worship leader does not equal Recording Artist
D.J. does not equal sound engineer.
Conference Speaker does not equal evangelist.
Prophetic does not equal prophet.
Decreeing & declaring does not equal apostle.
Knowledge does not equal advisor.
Aged does not equal deacon/deaconess.

Athletic does not equal coach.
Lawyer does not equal politician.
Objective does not equal counselor.
Articulate does not equal Lecturer.
Listener does not equal friend.
Team player does not equal team leader.
Poetic does not equal author.
Reporter does not equal columnist.
Wealth does not equal CEO.

Clever does not equal genius.
Socialite does not equal influencer.
Educated does not equal teacher.

Leaders, you are responsible for who you place where. When people are out of position, guess who suffers? The followers.

"Sometimes a person's gift grows faster than their maturity."
Bill Winston
Senior Pastor, Living Word Christian Center

note twelve:

rejection

*written to the leader
who has been discarded.*

"Rejection is neither an indication of value or talent. Remember that. If you believe in what you have to offer, then don't stop offering it simply because some of those you offer it to reject it. Many people are simply not very good at recognizing talent or value. It doesn't mean you won't eventually find an audience that will."

Zero Dean

On May 24, 1844, Samuel Morse sent the first telegram from Washington, D.C. to Baltimore, MD. It read, "What hath God wrought?" After this, the telegraph became the way to communicate long-distance using Morse Code. The electrical telegraph was a point-to-point text messaging system, used from the 1840s until better systems became widespread. It allowed people to transmit information over long distances by using coded pulses of electric currents through dedicated wires.

In 1876, Alexander Graham Bell had an even better idea, "What if one could hear the voice of the person they wished to communicate with?" He realized that he should partner with the company in control of the main method of communication at the time, and approached them to offer a patent. Western Union President William Orten responded to Alexander Graham Bell,

"After careful consideration of your invention, while it is a very interesting novelty, we have come to the conclusion

that it has no commercial possibilities. What use could this company make of an electrical toy?"

Bell had offered Orten the patent on his new invention, the telephone, for $100,000 (worth about $2M in current dollars). Two years later, after the telephone began to take off, Orten realized the magnitude of his mistake and spent years (unsuccessfully) challenging Bell's patents.

Many inventions derived from the telephone, such as a telephone network, exchanges, rotary dialing, payphones, touch-tone phones, cordless phones, cell phones, telephone books, caller ID, 911, etc. What state would the modern world be in had Bell thrown his patent in the garbage and walked away because he was rejected?

In 2006, Western Union shut down its telegraph service in the United States. At the time, the company reported that only about 20,000 telegrams had been sent in the previous year.

The telegram would officially be put to rest in July 2013, when the last large-scale telegraph system in the world stopped its service. India's state-run telecommunications company, Bharat Sanchar Nigam Limited (BSNL), sent its last telegram on July 14, 2013. The decision was made because the telegraph service was no longer commercially viable. Why was it no longer commercially viable? Because of smart phone texting. There was no longer a need for a telegram, because texting became mainstream.

We all have a William Orten in our lives, someone

who thinks our gift is worthless or no longer has value. But a leader still has vision in a dark room. For every William Orten, there are thousands who will see the value in your gifts, talents, and ideas. Instead of trying to convince people to believe in you and marketing yourself to people who compete with you, seek those who can find value in what you have, and are not competing for your lane.

Leaders, you will be rejected. Despite how hard you work, someone will scoff at your idea. However, you can't let your flame go out. You can't throw in the towel. You can't devalue yourself. And do not allow yourself to reject new ideas.

In 2020, including both smart and feature phones, the current number of mobile phone users is 4.78 billion, which makes 61.62% of people in the world a cell phone owner. And we are completely helpless without it.

"If you are someone who dislikes, condemns and rejects new ideas, you aren't fit to lead."

Israelmore Ayivor

note thirteen:

vengeance

written to the leader who desires retribution.

"I am convinced that imprisonment is a way of pretending to solve the problem of crime. It does nothing for the victims of crime, but perpetuates the idea of retribution, thus maintaining the endless cycle of violence in our culture..."

Howard Zinn

Have you ever been victimized? Has someone ever posted, printed, or proclaimed something about you to the masses that was completely inaccurate? Has an incorrect narrative been circulated about you? Have you ever felt like you were imprisoned by a perception? Have you ever made a mistake or had an issue in your life that people keep revisiting? Have you ever been the subject of a meeting you were not invited to? Have you ever had something unjustly taken from you either as a child or an adult? Have you ever wanted to get back at the person who took it, destroyed it, spread it, posted it, or texted it?

When these things happen to us, we toil with the question, "How am I'm going to handle this?" We spend time thinking of creative ways to repay the person who has defiled us. Our anger boils like water in a pot, and the lid can hardly contain the built-up pressure inside. We are ready to explode. We want to repay them...We want vengeance.

Our natural instinct is to answer enmity with enmity.

However, Proverbs 20:22 tells us, *"Do not say, 'I will avenge this evil!' Wait on the LORD, and He will deliver you."*

The Greek word for vengeance is *ekdikésis*, which means vindication, a defense, avenging, or full (complete) punishment.

To avenge is to punish a wrong-doing with the intent of seeking justice. Vengeance is personal, less concerned with justice. Vengeance is retaliation by inflicting harm.

Avenging is done by a third party. Vengeance/Revenge, however, is always done by the victim. Its aim is to ensure that the offender knows what it feels like to be victimized.

But in the spirit world, only God has the right to retaliate and recompense. This is why God states in Deuteronomy 32:35, *"Vengeance is mine, and recompense; Their foot shall slip in due time; For the day of their calamity is at hand, And the things to come hasten upon them.'"* God is the third party in the matter.

True vindication cannot come from you but must always come from a third party. In the spiritual instance, it is God. When we have been victimized, He will handle it.

To truly avenge, brings justice, not harm. It allows for healing, not pain. It results in restoration, not condemnation.

We have examples of this in the natural world. When a man or woman has been unjustly jailed or sent to prison for a crime they have not committed, their true freedom and vindication can't come from the prosecution or the defense. It must come from a third party that has no ties to either side, only the side of justice. Organizations like the Innocence Project, Center on Wrongful Convictions of Youth, Youth Represent, and The National Legal Aid & Defender Association, to name a few, are independent organizations that are not tied to either the prosecutor or the defense to bring justice to those that have been wrongly accused. They are avenging...not seeking revenge. Their work brings exaltation, healing, justice, and restoration to the person who was falsely accused.

We have to remember that wrong-doing WILL happen to you. It's not unavoidable. However, when people do you wrong, it does not always mean that they are evil. We have flesh. We have a sinful nature. We have tendencies and influencers. We have motives that are not always pure. We have thoughts that are not always sound. Many times, we respond with our emotions that, if unchecked, can drive us to insensibility.

There is a belief that if the person who wronged us also feels some pain, we will feel better. But studies have shown that this is not true.

A recent study published in the Journal of Personality and Social Psychology suggests that seeking revenge does temporarily make us feel better, but what does constant retaliation do to our long-term mental health?

"You may think that getting revenge will alleviate your

feelings of anger, but in fact, it seems to increase them." A 2008 research study by psychology professor Kevin Carlsmith found that when people exacted revenge, their anger lingered longer than in those who did not. "Carlsmith believed that this was due to ruminating on the incident, because it was taken to a heightened level of pain — that once a person crossed the line and exacted revenge on another, the situation was deemed more hurtful."

Revenge never allows you to forgive or forget. It never starts the healing process. Could this be one of the reasons why God said, "Vengeance is mine. I will repay."?

God not only wants to punish, when needed, but to avenge (seek justice). He wants to exonerate and then restore you. But you can't exonerate and restore yourself when you have been wrongly accused or been victimized. It must come from someone/someplace else...a third party.

Spending time in vengeance takes up too much of your mind-space and keeps you from moving forward. You are always looking back to what was done and pondering how you could have handled it differently. Vengeance keeps you imprisoned by your past. It causes you to never seek freedom, but always look back at why you became a prisoner.

It's in our DNA to do wrong and to want to retaliate, but we must stay calm. Think of people as fish, and you are a fisherman. The fisherman has the boat, the net, the pole, and the capability. But a fish will soon be caught in its own net.

> *"Look, Chief, you can't go off half-cocked looking for vengeance against a fish. That shark isn't evil. It's not a murderer. It's just obeying its own instincts. Trying to get retribution against a fish is crazy."*
>
> *Peter Benchley, Jaws*

note fourteen:

the deceiver

written to the leader who has been misled by an incorrect narrative unawares.

"Machiavelli did believe that it was better to appear to be good than to be good. If you're good, you're just too vulnerable, but if you appear to be good, you get all the benefits plus you can be sneaky and, when necessary, stab someone in the back."
David Ignatius

W e often think deception is used to defraud those who are subject to us, but it is actually used as a pretense to shift decision-makers. The true purpose behind deception is to maintain **access** to the authority figure.

Deception, in Webster's Revised Unabridged Dictionary, means "to deprive by stealth." A person who walks in deception will be unseen to the leader. Deceivers keep themselves cloaked by means of sophisticated communication that keeps the leader in a maze of emotional responses that produce predetermined outcomes.

Many leaders are under the influence of deception unawares. If they look hard enough, they will find deceivers amongst their paid staff, inner circle, board of directors, trustees, counsel of advisors, members, volunteers, students, mentees, spiritual children, and even family.

Our deceiver of interest in this note is a biblical character by the name of Jonadab. We meet Jonadab in 2 Samuel 13. He is King David's nephew (he is family). The

Bible says that Jonadab is an advisor/confidant (he has influence) of his cousin Amnon (King David's son). As a relative, he has (benefits) access to everything the king's family enjoys.

Jonadab advises Amnon to lure his sister Tamar to his residence by saying he's sick. Amnon lures Tamar in, rapes her, and casts her out of his house. Her brother, Absalom, comforts her and takes her into his home for two years. Let's read this story in 2 Samuel 13:3-6 (NIV).

"Now Amnon had an adviser named Jonadab son of Shimeah, David's brother. Jonadab was a very shrewd man. He asked Amnon, "Why do you, the king's son, look so haggard morning after morning? Won't you tell me?"
Amnon said to him, "I'm in love with Tamar, my brother Absalom's sister."
"Go to bed and pretend to be ill," Jonadab said. "When your father comes to see you, say to him, 'I would like my sister Tamar to come and give me something to eat. Let her prepare the food in my sight so I may watch her and then eat it from her hand.'"
So Amnon lay down and pretended to be ill. When the king came to see him, Amnon said to him, "I would like my sister Tamar to come and make some special bread in my sight, so I may eat from her hand."

In my first book, *The Cost of Indecision: A Plan for Music & Life*, I address the importance of understanding the meaning of your name. We are a product of our names. We carry the disposition and characteristics of the names we are given at birth. The second part of the name *Jonadab* comes from the verb in Hebrew *nadab*, meaning *to incite*. You may remember two brothers in Leviticus 10 named *Nadab* and Abihu, who **incited** the wrath of God by releasing strange fire in the tabernacle. *Nadab* and Abihu were the sons of Aaron (family) and had assigned duties in the tabernacle as priests to their uncle Moses (access). Because they released a strange (unauthorized) fire, God burned them alive. The fire of God consumed them from the inside, leaving their outside appearance unharmed.

In 2 Samuel 13, the Bible tells us that Jonadab was very *shrewd*, which means wily, crafty, and clever. Some translations also say that he was *subtle* (not immediately obvious or comprehensible; difficult to detect or analyze).

After the rape took place, King David heard about what happened and became furious (2 Samuel 13:21) but did nothing after he calmed. For two years, Amnon did not answer for his crime, as Absalom had instructed Tamar not to speak against her brother Amnon (2 Samuel 13:22).

Many leaders respond to situations in the same manner as King David. They become furious after hearing about an incident, but after anger subsides, go back to doing the work of the organization. The leader may fuss and even curse at their staff, members, associates, volunteers, and family. However, they don't speak to the perpetrator directly or ask questions to uncover the root of the situation.

Let's read 2 Samuel 13:30 – 35 (NIV). Take a closer look at how Jonadab spins his web with the king. He has planted the seed for rape, watched it take place, maintained stealth and silence in the cover-up, and kept his dealings from the king. At the opportune time, he surfaces with information to make himself appear honorable to the king.

"While they were on their way, the report came to David: "Absalom has struck down all the king's sons; not one of them is left." 31 The king stood up, tore his clothes and lay down on the ground; and all his attendants stood by with their clothes torn.

But Jonadab son of Shimeah, David's brother, said, "My lord should not think that they killed all the princes; only Amnon is dead. This has been Absalom's express intention ever since the day Amnon raped his sister Tamar. 33 My lord the king should not be concerned about the report that all the king's sons are dead. Only Amnon is dead."

Meanwhile, Absalom had fled.

Now the man standing watch looked up and saw many

people on the road west of him, coming down the side of the hill. The watchman went and told the king, "I see men in the direction of Horonaim, on the side of the hill."
Jonadab said to the king, "See, the king's sons have come; it has happened just as your servant said.""

David was so emotional about the report of his sons' murders that he was unable to think logically. Perhaps, had he been more focused, King David would have asked, *"If you (Jonadab, a relative with access to me) knew of my son's (Absalom) intentions to kill my son (Amnon) for two years, why didn't you alert me to stop this?"* Remember, the deceiver creates plots, watches them unfold, and maintains their stealth. At the right time, the deceiver will emerge so that they may be seen as a trusted confidant.

Since he had direct access to him, Jonadab got to King David first to report that only Amnon had been killed to control the narrative in David's emotional state. This kept the original scheme of his orchestrated rape covered.

The Jonadab's among you can always get in contact with you before anyone else. When they call, you will answer; when they Facetime, you will pick up; when they text, you will respond; when they email, you will reply. They don't have to set up meetings to talk with you. They can bypass security, secretaries, and armor bearers to update you on the latest news, gossip, secrets, and conversations to their benefit.

Why can they do this? Because the leader has created an environment for Jonadab to exist. They know you will believe them. After all, they are trusted, they are family, they are considered "sons" and "daughters", they are staff, and only a limited amount of people have direct access to you. Jonadab knows you won't have the clarifying conversation to get to the bottom of the chaos they create. They have observed you and learned that you are a passive-aggressive leader. They are aware that once you are no longer emotionally distraught, you will go right back to your desk and do nothing. Jonadab has also recognized your tolerance for gossip. You may comment on the news Jonadab reports, but you won't confront it. You, the leader, have created the perfect environment for Jonadab to thrive.

Many leaders have Jonadab's among them. The very person who has conspired division in the house and caused you to weep is sometimes the same person who will bring you good news to console you all the while keeping themselves cloaked and using deception to maintain their access.

"Men are so simple and so much inclined to obey immediate needs that a deceiver will never lack victims for his deceptions."

Niccolo Machiavelli

note fifteen:

succession

Written to the leader who struggles with retiring.

"I hated all my work that I labored at under the sun because I must leave it to the man who comes after me. And who knows whether he will be a wise man or a fool? Yet he will take over all my work that I labored at skillfully under the sun. This too is futile. So I began to give myself over to despair concerning all my work that I had labored at under the sun. When there is a man whose work was done with wisdom, knowledge, and skill, and he must give his portion to a man who has not worked for it, this too is futile and a great wrong."

Ecclesiastes 2:18-21 (HCSB)

It seems natural for leaders who have invested their lives to build something to lament the fact that someone else must eventually step into their shoes. Someone who may not handle the institution correctly; someone who may not cherish what has been constructed; someone who may not have the intellect and insight to maintain the accumulation of wealth, property, and territory and propel it into the future. These are both valid and understandable concerns for any leader. However, to avoid uncertainty and increase the survival rate of their life's work, leaders must see the value in selecting, preparing, and training a successor.

As he oversaw the construction of the temple and his royal palace for twenty years, Solomon gathered great wealth and wisdom. Solomon was not only the wisest man in the world but also the richest. (2 Chronicles 9:22) Unfortunately, because of his disobedience, all of Solomon's hard work and accomplishments would be inherited, not by his sons, but by his servant. Solomon had disobeyed God and had broken the mandate of God by marrying foreign wives, being influenced by them, and worshipping and building shrines to the Moabite and Ammonite gods. The Lord became angry with Solomon because his heart had turned from the God of Israel. The Lord said to Solomon in 1 Kings 11:11, *"Because you have done this, and have not kept My covenant and My statutes, which I have commanded you, I will surely tear the kingdom away from you and give it to your servant. Nevertheless I will not do it in your days, for the sake of your father David; I will tear it out of the hand of your son."*

God's decision concerning Solomon's legacy and the writer's frustration about his legacy depicted in Ecclesiastes 2:18-21 show leaders the value in pinpointing and developing successors and how we must handle the assignments given to us so that what has been built will not be destroyed.

As leaders, we must understand that the survival of what we have built relies on how we train the potential successor. Before he stepped down as CEO of Apple, Steve Jobs prepared his succession plan in the form of Apple University. Founded in 2008, Apple University has a leadership curriculum with content and materials based on Job's experiences. Its purpose is to teach Apple employees how to think like Steve Jobs and make decisions that he would make.

This digital curriculum set up by Jobs is a great example of how technology can be used to prepare a company's leadership succession.

Besides Apple University, Steve Jobs also worked hard to prepare Tim Cook for the position of CEO. Cook took on a variety of different operational roles including manufacturing, distribution, sales, and supply chain management before working directly with Jobs to gain experience in the CEO role. The first thing you notice is that Jobs identified a successor. Second, he prepared him for the role of CEO by having him learn every facet of the company he would eventually run. Thirdly, Cook sat with Jobs and gleaned from him directly and intentionally. Jobs imparted into Cook what was in him.

In his resignation letter, Steve Jobs wrote, *"As far as my successor goes, I strongly recommend that we execute our succession plan and name Tim Cook as CEO of Apple."*

In a recent interview, Tim Cook shared his view on succession planning saying, *"I see my role as CEO to prepare as many people as I can to be CEO, and that's what I'm doing. And then the board makes a decision at that point in time."*

Apple has seen the importance of having a proper succession plan in place to ensure that there are no transitional issues when it comes to leadership and succession in the company.

Leaders, face the fact that you won't be in your current position forever. Whether through resignation, firing, or death, your time as the leader will come to an end. You must put procedures in place to ensure that successors are always being trained and prepared. It is also important to identify individuals who can get hands-on training directly from you. In addition to being prepared to take over, they also need to be evaluated to make sure they have what it takes to lead.

Don't end up like the writer in Ecclesiastes who resented the work he put into his legacy because he was unsure of the competence of his successor. Likewise, don't end up like Solomon, who, because of his decisions, was not able to chose who his successor would be, and lost all the profit he accumulated.

As a leader, you should never leave the company, organization, ministry, association, etc., in the hands of uncertainty. Legacy is developed when you are in position, but sustained by your ability to plan for your leave. Your success plan starts with YOU.

"One of the things we often miss in succession planning is that it should be gradual and thoughtful, with lots of sharing of information and knowledge and perspective, so that it's almost a non-event when it happens."

Anne M. Mulcahy

acknowledgments

As with many acknowledgments, you find a long list of people that are thanked who, most times, have never met the author or knew they even made an impact on them. I won't bore you with that. However, as with all acknowledgments, you thank the people who helped you complete your book.

I thank God for allowing me to complete a second book and for giving me the ability to speak and explain topics plain and clear. I thank my parents for all of their support, encouragement, and acts of kindness. I thank my one and only sibling, Daniel, the greatest musician in the world, for being a great brother, husband, and father. I thank my beautiful and amazing daughter, Mackenzie. You are such a gift, and I can't imagine life without you. You inspire me and keep me going, and I thank you for being such a thoughtful child.

I'd like to thank Jessica Williams and Keen Vision Publishing for all that you've done to assist me in getting this book completed. You, Jessica, have been such a blessing. Thank you, Pastor John Hannah, for simply caring about me, the individual. I want to thank Dr. Pam Ross for her excellence in Leadership Development and her contribution to this book. You have produced leaders in every sector, from Business to Religion. Thank you, Gina Waters Miller, for your outstanding grace and leadership in the Music Industry. You stand tall, and your light shines bright.

To every conference coordinator, ministry, pastor, and artist that allowed me to speak to your organization/team, thank you. To every leader who reached out to me personally for advice on how to handle tough issues, thank you. It sharpened me to add context to this book. To all those I mentor, thank you for choosing me to develop you. I hope that I have made your life better.

I want to thank everyone in the Music and Fine Arts departments at Valley Kingdom Ministries International and All Nations Worship Assembly Headquarters and its affiliates that allowed me to lead you.

Finally, I want to acknowledge the purchaser and reader of this book. I hope that all I have shared makes you a better leader regardless of what area your leadership lies in and equips you to become a better steward of those who are entrusted to your care.

about the author

Michael Weatherspoon has been in the music industry for 30 years as a drummer, producer, consultant and label executive. Forming Spoonfed Productions with his brother Daniel Weatherspoon 20 years ago has produced dozens of records for various gospel and inspirational artists around the world. Having performing on over 100 albums and DVDs during his career and touring with dozens of artists and presenting at music conferences, Michael has gained valuable knowledge, insight, and experience to help new and seasoned artists achieve their goals in their career.

In April 2016, Michael released a book entitled, The Cost of Indecision that deals with Levitical Practices on how to properly manage, supervise, organize and structure ministries in the church. Michael has spoken to several church music & leadership departments, gospel artists, leadership & music conferences on the importance of Order in music, leadership and church ministry around the country. Michael served as Minister of Music at Valley Kingdom Ministries International (Chicago) and as Pastor of Worship at All Nations Worship Assembly (Chicago). He also served as president of The Well Media Group.

Currently, Michael is on the Board of Directors for American Blues Theater, one of Chicago's premier musical theater companies, and the Development Committee with Porch Light Musical Theater Company.

stay connected

Thank you for reading, *Notes to a Leader*. Michael looks forward to connecting with you and keeping you updated on his next releases. Below are a few ways you can connect with the author.

FACEBOOK @MWeatherspoon
INSTAGRAM @michaelweatherspoon
TWITTER @michaeljspoon
EMAIL info@michaelweatherspoon.com
WEBSITE www.michaelweatherspoon.com